Wrapped in Faith

KAREN BOLDEN

Trilogy Christian Publishers
A Wholly Owned Subsidary of Trinity Broadcasting Network
2442 Michelle Drive
Tustin, CA 92780

Cover Photograph by Alex Laroco; Graphics by Nathaniel Williamsom

For information, address Trilogy Christian Publishing
Rights Department, 2442 Michelle Drive, Tustin, Ca 92780.
Trilogy Christian Publishing/ TBN and colophon are trademarks of Trinity Broadcasting Network.

For information about special discounts for bulk purchases, please contact Trilogy Christian Publishing.

Manufactured in the United States of America

Trilogy Disclaimer: The views and content expressed in this book are those of the author and may not necessarily reflect the views and doctrine of Trilogy Christian Publishing or the Trinity Broadcasting Network.

10 9 8 7 6 5 4 3 2 1

Library of Congress Cataloging-in-Publication Data is available.

ISBN 978-1-63769-030-7 (Print Book)
ISBN 978-1-63769-031-4 (ebook)

This book is dedicated to anyone who has been given a diagnosis of cancer.

Receiving a diagnosis of cancer can be a major blow, which can bring on a lot of emotions such as denial, anger, anxiety, loneliness, hatred, restlessness, resentment, hopelessness—all that needs to be processed and worked out. Once I went through my own process (everyone is different), it enabled me to see where I stood in my faith walk with God. To get to that point, I had to ask myself some hard questions. Questions such as "where is my faith?" "whom do I place my trust in?" We are all at different levels of faith. The Bible tells us, "faith is the substance of things hoped for, the evidence of things not seen" (Hebrews 11:1 NKJV).

That substance is a reality in which we are praying and looking forward to manifesting itself into a state of being, regardless of what our situation may look like at the present time. It really does not matter to what degree of faith one may or may not have because God's Word says that if we have faith the size of a mustard seed, we can move a mountain (Matthew 17:20 NKJV). I understand that a mustard seed is one of the tiniest seeds, yet when it grows, it is greater than the herbs, and it becomes a tree.

This life is a faith walk no matter what we are going through. God requires it from us. The Bible tells us, "the just shall live by faith; but if anyone draws back My soul has no pleasure in him" (Hebrews 10:28 NKJV). "But without faith, it is impossible to please Him, for he who comes to

God, must believe that He is and He is a rewarder of those who diligently seek Him" (Hebrews 11:6 NKJV).

Faith is an action word and requires us to act. You may ask, "how do I put faith into action?" We put our faith into action first of all, by acknowledging God as the ultimate physician. We trust Him that He leads us to the appropriate medical team to care for us. We must remember that "death and life are in the power of the tongue" (Proverbs 18:21 NKJV).

Be careful what comes out of your mouth, speaking only positive affirmations over your health. A few examples:

> *"I am healed by the stripes of Jesus."*
> *"No weapon formed against me shall prosper."*
> *"I am an overcomer."*
> *"My name is victory."*

Declare your healing no matter what it looks like, be an encourager to others who are going through similar situations. Participate in speaking engagements when asked.

If you do not know Jesus as your Lord and Savior, I pray you take this time to pray this prayer:

> "Lord, I believe in my heart and confess with my mouth that Your Son Jesus died for my sins. He was buried and raised on the third day and now seated at Your right hand, making intercessions for me. I invite You into my heart to be my Lord and Savior. Forgive me of my sins and cleanse me from all unrighteousness in Jesus' name. *Amen!*"

I pray that my story will empower you, giving you hope to walk in faith for your healing. It is not over until God says so.

CONTENTS

ACKNOWLEDGEMENTS

To God, my Father, the only Father I have ever really known. Words cannot express my feelings of who and all You are to me. I believe that all who read my story can and will appreciate this statement.

To my Beautiful Redeemer family—if your name is not mentioned in this book, just know that you are all a part of my family. When medical advice was given to me to protect my immune system and stay away from anyone who did not feel well, you respected that. Yet, when I needed hugs, prayers, and words of encouragement, you gave freely. Thank you, Pastor Mike, sister Jackie for all that you do for the ministry, looking over your flock to keep us whole. The occasional dinners you and the Liggins (Carla and Danny) family provided to give Ron a break was so thoughtful. While Danny has since passed, I must express my feelings for his support. I will remember him as my brother in Christ, and his encouragement helped me so much, especially when he was going through his own health issues. To Dr. David Wren, my teacher, who always give me sound advice that was scripturally based, along with medical advice. For all of your continued prayers, I feel and appreciate so much.

To Cynthia Taylor. I thank you for a great impact on my life. You came to visit and brought with you something I still hold dear. That was the Charles Capps little book called *God's Creative Power For Healing*. You sat down with me and read through a few pages before you left. I, however, continued with reading the entire little book and felt so empowered. I still use this book, and I give it as gifts to others in the hope they too will come away feeling the same.

To my co-worker at Drs Medical Center, Rachelle Bradley who was my co-worker before becoming my manager. You were always supportive, and you still are. Thank you.

To Karen Davis and Penny Berry. I will never forget how you both came to the rescue and stood by me, holding my hand while the radiologist performed the breast needle localization prior to my surgery. It was very painful, and you allowed me to use your hands to squeeze. That's just one incident, but there were many more examples of your support.

To Jinny Choi, my co-worker, office mate for the past five years, and now one of my managers at Kaiser. It has been a pleasure working with you, and I thank you for your support in so many areas. A listening ear, an encourager, and support system to become "*kaisurized.*" Thanks, Jin!

To Adrian Boyance Reid and Nancy Cadet, my former co-workers, and former manager respectively who has now become my walking mates. Thanks for being part of my life. I really enjoy our breakfasts, conversations, and exercise, although lately it's been difficult to do due to the pandemic. Thanks, ladies!

To my prayer warriors and Zoom group:

Berney K Dorton, who I have known since elementary school. My co-worker, my friend, my sister in Christ, and a mighty "prayer warrior." Thank you for being there for me and my family. I love you.

Diane Newman, the Godmother of my oldest child, my friend who I consider a sister, as well as my sister in Christ. Thank you for always being there for me and having a listening ear. I love you.

Linda Conley, the Godmother of my youngest child. We called ourselves sisters back in Jr High, and we still do. Thank you for being there for me, supporting me with prayer, and for the continued close relationship with Bri. I love you.

To Cheryl Winfield, I have cherished our friendship over these past forty-four years. Mark was just two years of age when we met at Mervyn's Department Store. Thank you for your support. I love you.

To Yolanda Mansfield, "Yo," thank you for asking me to be Keandra's Godmother. The years we shared watching our daughters grow up together are memorable. Our sisterhood, our friendship, and your support through everything mean so much to me. Thank you for always being there for me, no matter what time of the day. I love you.

To Wanda Braddy, my mentor in Christ, who didn't give me my first haircut, but you did give me my first shave (smile). Thank you for your loving support and your prayers. I love you.

To Leona Welch, another mighty woman of God who has shown so much support with a listening ear and words of encouragement. I love you.

To my family, who I am sure will understand if I do not list you all. Our family is so large that I am sure I will forget someone. From my grandchildren to my nieces, nephews, cousins, in-laws—you know that I love each and every one of you, and I'm so thankful to have you in my life.

My children, Charles Jr, Markus, Brienne, and Cameron. Words cannot express how much I love you. A parent does the best he or she can to raise a child. While there may be a lot of parenting books out on the market, no one guide book fits all, except one. The best guide I know now, but not back then, is what the Word of God says: to "train up a child in the way he should go, and when he is old, he will not depart from it" (Proverbs 22:6 NKJV). I was eighteen years old when I had June, just a child myself. I basically grew up with you all. There were many times I wondered if I was being too strict and old-fashioned. All I knew was I loved you and was determined not to lose you to the streets. Now that you are grown, I feel that God has blessed me with children who have endured a lot through divorces and my health issues. You remain strong and encouraging to me and for me. You are there if I need you without hesitation. My one and only prayer now is for all of you to have a relationship with God. Some of you do already, and the others know who you are. This prayer is an act of my faith in operation, declaring it over your lives that it will manifest itself in due season. I love you.

FOREWORD

Resolute: characterized by firmness and determination, as the temper, spirit, actions, etc.

I once asked my mother if she ever considered medical marijuana as an option for treatments...her response... let's just say if looks could kill.

I can only imagine how terrified she must have been each time a scan resulted in concern.

However, she embraced her courage, faced those challenges with her own health and of other family members, and persevered.

Her faith and trust in God and devotion to family are undaunting and unwavering. In other words...resolute

Charles Douglas Jr.

Resilient. That's the best Word I can think of to describe my mother. All that she has been through. The pain. Waiting on scan results. The surgeries. The treatments. The loss of loved ones... If she ever lost her faith in the Lord, she never showed it. Through it all, she has maintained her relationship with God when others might question why things are happening to them. She inspires me to stay positive when I am not at my best.

Markus Douglas

Loving, caring, beautiful, loyal, strict... (sometimes too strict), and faithful are just a few thoughts of how I view my mother. Her story *Wrapped in Faith* exemplifies 1 Corinthians 2:5, "as she demonstrates what it looks like to walk in faith." I am proud to call her my mother, and I pray that those who read her journey will be inspired, as I have, to continue to be strong in your faith walk as God holds your hand and guides you.

Brienne Douglas

Karen Bolden is a Beautiful woman that goes out of her way to do a lot for people. As I have grown, it's become more apparent the big hand she has played in my life. Through her struggles, many would have turned many directions. But my auntie stayed the straight and narrow way of God. Yeah, the past years have been emotional, but the strength that comes… you couldn't get out without the struggle. There is beauty in the struggle, and all I want is for my aunt to see me on top of the game.

Cameron Fulton

Breast cancer? No way! This must be a dream! I am a child of the Most High God; I give Him the first fruit of my day. I give Him praise with my lips. I talk the talk, and I walk the walk.

I am the go-to person when others need prayer. I am an advocate when others seek medical attention. This cannot be happening to me! Someone pinch me so I can wake up cause I am not feeling this at all. Oh my goodness, it's not a dream. What happened? Did I fall from grace? Abba Father, where are You?

INTRODUCTION

When you hear statistics that one out of every seven women will develop breast cancer, you pray that one person isn't you. I happen to be that one out of seven. I'm sure that every woman diagnosed with breast cancer felt as I did when I was given the news—a feeling of shock, disbelief, scared, or maybe a little angry. I even went so far as to tell God, "Lord, I'm a believer, I praise and worship You, I study Your Word, I am there for everyone else. How can this happen to me?" Then I heard the Holy Spirit say to me, "you are not exempt." Wow! What I gleam from that is that now I have to apply my faith in God's Word to my situation and take it one day at a time. I am not saying that this journey was easy at all. I understand that God allows us to be tested through situations. If you have read the Book of Job, you clearly understand this. Satan could not do what he did to Job without God's permission. So it is with us. God knows what we are going to go through before it even happens. The Bible says that we are going to have trials and tribulations but that He does not give us more than we can bear.

1 Peter 5:10 tells us that after we have suffered a while, God will perfect, establish, strengthen, and settle us. This lets me know that through all of my struggles, God is there to help mold me where I am able to stand firm, be immovable, and, most of all, victorious.

Lord, I thank You for everything. You have been with me from the beginning and continue to show me that You are always near. Even when I felt alone, I knew that I wasn't.

Your Spirit not only lives in me but surrounds me with the beautiful people that you keep sending in my path. Powerful praying, encouraging, uplifting people is needed to help weather any storm. I pray to be an example for You, Lord, to let Your light shine in me even in the midst of bad situations, showing others that You hold all power in Your hand and that You have the final say in *every* situation. It is up to us to stand on Your Word and leave the rest to You. In Jesus' name, *Amen*!

CHAPTER 1

It was a usual weekday morning, so I thought. I had just completed my Bible reading, some meditation, and thanking God for the day. I placed my books on top of my headboard and proceeded to bring my hands down when my right hand just slid down right over my right breast, landing on a lump. I sprung forth immediately with my mind racing. I felt for it again sitting upright, no lump, I laid back down, there it is! *Oh no, Oh no*, kept racing through my mind. I took a few deep breaths, climbed out of bed, and proceeded to get ready for work. I told my husband, Ron, that I found a lump in my breast and that I was going to follow up with it at work that morning and left. I said it so nonchalant and fast that he did not have any time for questions, and I was not in any mood to answer any at the time, so I went off in a hurry.

I work at a local hospital where I am a Registered Nurse with two and a half years of medical surgical experience, twenty-one years of intensive care experience, and now working as a Case Manager/Discharge Planner for the past eight years.

Upon arrival at work, I proceeded to organize my day and tried to make an appointment with my OBGYN's office. I was told that my doctor was busy due to a backlog in her surgery schedule. I was getting frustrated with the office nurse because I felt if a patient tells you that she found a lump, she should get priority. That is not the case and was not the case for me. I was told that if I wanted to, I could come and sit and wait to be seen that afternoon, which I decided I would do. In the meantime, I paged my primary doctor, found him in the medical staff office, and went to see him. I explained the morning incidence of what and how I found the lump. He called and ordered an ultrasound of my breast and told me, "everything is going to be okay." I love my doctor; he is not only an intelligent man but a truly caring person. I went through the proper procedures to register for the ultrasound and calmly went back to work. By midafternoon, I had not been called for the ultrasound test, so I called the department to be told they were backed up with outpatients, and I would probably have to be done another day. I calmly told the tech that I might be an employee, but I was also an outpatient who had registered properly and have been waiting my turn. She took me right then and performed the procedure. I knew something was not right when she stated she was going to have a doctor come and look at the screen. Sure enough, after viewing the screen, the doctor said that I needed a biopsy which was scheduled forthe following week.

I took some deep breaths, said internally, "Okay God, it's You and me," and went back to work with so many thoughts and emotions running through my mind; I needed to figure out what and if to tell my family members anything. I did tell my husband, Ron, and told him not to say anything until I had a chance to pray about it. I wanted to wait to tell my children after I had more information. My sister Mae was dealing with some personal problems with our nephew, and she really did not need to have anything else on her plate. She was in the process of something major with him. My other sister Mal was in remission from ovarian cancer, diagnosed two years earlier; therefore, it was God and me.

I had the biopsy approximately four days later, and within two days, I received a call telling me that I had cancer. I was in shock, and the tears begin to flow. Immediate plans got underway with picking a surgeon the same day. The first MD that was recommended was changed by me as I chose another physician.

I had Ron call my children to inform them of this diagnosis because I was not in a position to speak with them at the present time. I have three children from a previous marriage for twelve and a half years: Charles Jr, Markus, and Brienne. All three grown college graduates and living on their own. Charles (who I call either June or Pillhead) and Markus still reside in California, and Bri lives in Arizona. We are raising our nephew, Cameron, who has been living with us since age seven, who had to be told as well. I am not quite sure how my kids were dealing with this, especially being told over the phone. They sounded okay, but I think they were trying to be strong for me. Cameron, on the other hand, I found in his bathroom crying over the sink. When I asked him what was wrong, he cried harder, saying, "you have cancer." All I could do was hug him and say as positive as I could that I would be alright. Ron has two sons, Ron Jr and Reggie, from his first marriage that we shared the news with as well. Next to tell was my mother, my sisters Mae and Mallory. That was hard to do because of their own personal issues I have already mentioned. I do have three other siblings, Wayne, Nadine, and James (Stevie). However, our relationships are most times a little strained and not as close as they should be. Now that the key family members have been informed, it was time to move on with the business at hand, which was my upcoming surgery.

Upon my first meeting with the surgeon, I had questions such as the fact that my mammogram results on my last one taken approximately five months ago were negative, yet I find this lump. My information card mailed to me said I was okay, yet the MD's report says I have "dense breast." Why was I not told of having dense breast? What other measures should have been taken knowing I had dense breast? Now that I have been diagnosed, I wanted to be scanned from head to toe to check on the rest of my body since the mammogram did not pick this up. My surgeon could not tell me the difference between the previous mammogram and the one after the biopsy. I also wanted my left breast checked, so I had an MRI of my breasts as well. I was proactive for myself at this point, and I had put on my nursing hat. After all, I am now in a fight for my life. My left breast was fine, and the total body scan was negative for any other signs of cancer.

Once again, I cried to the Lord, "Lord, I praise You, I get up every morning reading and meditating on Your Word. I am there for others in medical crisis; I pray with them, go to their doctor appointments with them, I give them Your words with scripture to encourage them! You know this! Why is this happening to me"? Once again, I heard the Holy Spirit say to me, "you are not exempt." Then I realized, "who do I think I am?" God reminded me of my book I had just completed, *Karen's Anointed Expressions Presents "Blessed."* This is my first book, which is a compilation of visual images that God had given to me over the years to express who He is. The images speak for themselves, included with printed capture, followed by a scripture. The images all deal with faith in God with lots of food for thought for each individual reader to examine where they are in their life. The image that I am referring to in particular right now for me is the one called "Calling on Jesus," with the cell phone as the visual. The main point in this visual is that we find it easier to trust God for minor illnesses than for something major such as cancer. We need to trust Him for everything. I had just signed on with a self-publishing company before my diagnosis and was in the middle of editing, and responding back and forth with the company, and going off to surgery for a lumpectomy.

Well, I had the lumpectomy about two weeks after the biopsy since I had the MRI and Pet Scans done prior to the procedure. I did well during the surgery. I was told that I had what they call triple-negative cancer, which they describe as an aggressive form of cancer that does not respond to Estrogen, Progesterone, and HER2 receptors. In other words, I would not be able to take the hormone therapy drugs post-chemotherapy that women who were tested positive for the hormone receptors. These hormone therapy drugs are used to either lower estrogen levels or stop estrogen from acting on breast cancer cells.

I decided that I wanted a second opinion on my medical treatment. I had gone to what they call Tumor Board where your case is presented to other surgeons, oncologist, radiologist, nurses, and hear them come up with a plan of care for you. They were aware that I would be seeing another surgeon in the Bay area that is well known and stated they would love to know what her opinion was. My initial treatment plan was for four weeks of two IV chemotherapy drugs called Adriamycin and Cytoxan. This would be followed by radiation and twelve weeks of a third chemo drug called Taxol. The second opinion agreed that this plan was a good one, so I proceeded.

I told my oncologist that I was a believer, and I was trusting that I was not going to have a difficult time with this treatment. I told him that I was going to work while under treatment. He looked at me and said, "let's get you through the first three sessions, and if you feel okay, we will let you go to work." Well, it did not turn out the way I thought. I felt so bad after the first session that I had to come back to the hospital for IV hydration the next morning. I was so sick; I could not believe it. I thought, okay, *that's why my doctor said what he said*, and I never talked about going to work after that. It took the grace of God to strengthen me through this along with my family, church family, friends, powerful praying saints, cards, visits, spiritual music made up for me, scripture readings. It gave me the strength to get off the couch or out of the bed, put on some clothes, turn on my walkman, and walk the court that I live on. By forcing myself to do this, listening to uplifting, spiritual songs of praises to God, enabled me to come back home feeling more like a human being. I really discovered that I received strength and energy whenever I did this routine and not allowing myself to stay in bed or on the couch having a pity party.

CHAPTER 2

I completed my first four rounds of a double combination of chemotherapy drugs, which ended at the end of May 2008. I was waiting for my three-week rotation to start the third chemotherapy drug when I felt a small painful area on the inner aspect of my incision. I thought, *wow, why is this hurting?* I happen to be on the phone with a co-worker at the time. I told her I needed to go and follow up on this. I initially tried to reach my surgeon, which was very hard to do. I was scheduled to go in and have my IV (PICC) dressing changed that morning in the oncology department, so I went in and had my oncologist look at it. He felt it and said he would go and see if he could contact my surgeon. In less than ten minutes, both the surgeon and oncologist appeared. It was decided that I would return to surgery the next day for a biopsy, all the time reassuring me that it probably was scar tissue since cancer does not hurt.

I decided not to tell my family about the biopsy. I did not want to worry them. I am not used to being the one who is in need of medical support. I am the one in the family that is there for everyone else. Ron brought me to the procedure the next day. I was awake during the whole procedure, again, still being told that it is probably scar tissue. I returned to the recovery room, where Ron was waiting for me. After what I felt was a sufficient amount of time for my surgeon to come and speak to me, I told Ron that this was not a good sign, that the doctor was taking too long to return. Sure enough, when he returned, he told me that he had not only been to the lab but that he has also gone to see my oncologist because they found that I still had cancer growing in me. He suggested that I ask the physician, who was my second opinion, to take over my case in which I had no problem with, and was going to do so anyway at that point.

I had a choice of having a mastectomy with reconstruction surgery or going ahead with the mastectomy and having reconstruction later. I chose not to wait for reconstruction surgery as it would delay my surgery. I would have had to wait for a consultation with the plastic surgeon, who would have to have the same opening in his surgery schedule as my breast surgeon. No way was I going to delay this procedure any longer!

I went to surgery in June, a few days before Father's Day, and actually came home on Father's Day with tubes and drains in tow. Recovery time was uneventful, not much pain as I had a "pain buster pump" connected to me. After healing from the second surgery, I believe it was a total of two weeks; I started on my third chemotherapy medication, which was scheduled once a week for twelve weeks. This medication was more tolerable, I guess, because it was at a smaller dose and every week. I got into a routine of exercise, walking up and down my street, juicing fruits and vegetables, trying to change my diet habits, reading a lot, educating myself. I also got involved in speaking engagements for breast cancer awareness while still under treatment. I continued to work on my book. I had my first book signing at my church, which was so nice for me. I was able to tell everyone that the book that God birth through me was preparing me for what I was going to go through. It's about our faith level in God and recognizing God for who He is in our lives, whether we trust Him above all things, or do we make our problems bigger than Him.

CHAPTER 3

Since I had the mastectomy, my radiologist oncologist determined that I did not need radiation since I had a total mastectomy. I was not comfortable with this decision, so I sought a second opinion recommended by my second surgeon. It was determined by my second opinion that I needed the radiation since I still had cancer through four rounds of major chemotherapy. I went back to the first radiation oncologist with this information because she was closer to home, and I did not want to have to travel so far every day for twenty-eight days to be followed by the second. I would have done so if the first MD did not agree to treat me. She stated that she understood, especially under the circumstances mentioned. I proceeded with radiation treatments halfway through the twelve weeks of chemotherapy. The combination of chemotherapy and radiation really wore me out. I was completely exhausted; however, determined to persevere.

CHAPTER 4

Further into my treatment schedule, I developed some lumps on the inner aspect of my right upper arm. At this point, I was told that any bump or lump should be checked out. I was scheduled for outpatient surgery to have them removed and analyzed. Again, I kept this from my family until after the procedure was over. I wanted to wait until the results were back before I said anything to my children. It did not work out that way because my sons dropped by the house that afternoon of the procedure. I could not pick up my grandson because my arm was a little tender. Of course, then I had to share the course of the morning with them. They clearly could see something was up. It was proven to be fatty tissue, thank God! This was the second time that I made a decision to protect my family from every little crisis until the procedure was over. I do not like worrying my family, as I mentioned before. I have this sense of protection and always will because I love them so much.

I completed my therapy in October 2009 and celebrated by going to Arizona to visit my daughter Brienne, accompanied by my mother and sister Mae. We had a nice visit; however, I was really exhausted from chemotherapy and radiation. I was determined to have a good time especially since mom and Mae were able to help me celebrate my birthday while there. We spent time with my aunt Lois and her son David and his family. This was special because I did not spend much time with aunt Lois growing up. She is my deceased father's baby sister, and since I was not raised by my father, I did not see his side of the family very much at all. From what I can recall, the time period of seeing anyone from his family was about ten years of age until present. It was not until Brienne moved to Phoenix for college that we reconnected after so many years. In fact, I still have not met aunt Lois's daughter, as she lives in another state.

CHAPTER 5

I returned home with plans to go on a Jazz Cruise that was scheduled for November and planned before I was diagnosed with cancer. I was reluctant to go because I was exhausted. My oncologist encouraged me to go stating I had been through a lot, treat myself, just relax, and use wheelchair service—all of which I did. I left the ship only once, and that was for an hour. It was relaxing listening to jazz, pacing myself between eating, sleeping, and going to the shows. It was just the right pace for my husband, Ron, as well since he was recovering from bilateral knee surgery the year prior to my diagnosis. He decided to have both knees done at the same time because he was told that they both were equally bad. If he did one at a time, the unoperated side would not be able to support the operative side. Since he was retired from working as a school administer, it made sense to go ahead and have both knees done at the same time. He did it on February 26th, 2007, the day after his birthday. I remember sitting in the waiting room for hours, waiting for him to come out. When he finally got to his room, it was about 8:00 p.m. As a nurse, I immediately noticed that his left arm was just lying limp by his side, like a stroke patient. He had limited movement with it. I mentioned it to his nurse, who followed up with his MD. They would have to run some tests the next day. He also suffered nerve damage in his right leg, which included a lot of swelling, pain, and a condition called "foot drop." The arm situation quickly corrected itself; the neurologist following Ron never admitted verbally that he

might have had a small stroke but did say that it would take one or two years for the nerves to regenerate in his right leg or maybe longer. He needed two weeks of inpatient rehab in a rehab facility before coming home. He has had a very slow recovery, moving from using a walker to a cane, and now able to walk without any device. However, he clearly walks like a penguin (smile). That year was my year to take care of him, driving him to his therapy and MD appointments. The hardest part was encouraging him to do the prescribed exercises that he was instructed to do at home. He was not one to do exercises on a daily basis. Even when he went to rehab, he would rather talk more than work. Well, we made it through the rest of the year of 2007 and celebrated by going on a jazz cruise that November. Ron was able to maneuver with his cane, taking a lot of sitting breaks and wheelchair when appropriate. Then as explained, he recovered enough to be able to drive himself around, improving slowly over time. Then January of 2008, it was his turn to take care of me through my journey as described earlier.

I returned to work the following January 2009 in remission, doing well. I continued to encourage other cancer patients, working on promoting my book and thanking God every day for my healing.

CHAPTER 6

My Journey Continues

My follow-up care involved Pet scans (body scans) every three months to keep a check on my status. Remember, I was not able to take any supplemental therapy and, at the time, was told there was no clinical trial study for me. I remained clear until my September scan showed two small lesions in my right lung. Needless to say, I was shocked and felt like I was hit in the stomach. I was told the lesions were too small to biopsy at that time. I insisted on another scan the following month, with no changes in the lesions. It was determined that I should wait two to three months to avoid too much radiation. I waited until the first week of January as recommended. The scan showed a third lesion, which meant we needed to take action. I had the lung biopsy, which landed me in the ICU with a partially collapsed lung requiring a chest tube in place for one day. It turned out that the biopsy proved to be cancer. My journey continues. My schedule this time would be a two-drug combination of Taxol and Avastin every three weeks. This time I was able to work two weeks on and take the week off of chemotherapy. I was scheduled on Mondays, which would give me a complete week to recuperate. I completed this regime in August. My scans showed that my lung was clear; however, I had a Hilum lymph node in my chest area that kept lighting up. I had heard about a procedure called Cyberknife radiation that delivers high dose radiation to difficult areas and only requires one to five treatments. I went for a consultation at UCSF. However, I was told that Cyberknife was not an option for me because it was too close to my heart and that there was a possibility of freezing my right lung. The doctor did tell me that if I were his wife, mother, sister, or daughter, he would recommend another type of radiation (IMRT) that could be done at my own place of employment. I pursued this with my radiation oncologist, and the plan was set for twenty-eight treatments. She felt that the lesions were so small, and the calibrations for the amount of radiation needed was very favorable not to affect too much surrounding tissue. I completed the therapy able to work during treatment. God is so good!

CHAPTER 7

I started developing headaches during radiation. I was not ignoring them, just monitoring them, yet I found myself taking more Tylenol and Excedrin than usual for me. I mentioned it to my primary physician one day while at work. He told me if it kept up for another week, we need to check it out. That got me concerned. I probably waited more than a week, as I am a little fuzzy about things at this point. I finally had an MRI of the brain, to be told a day later that there were indeed two small lesions. One in the left temporal area and one in the left cerebellar area of my brain. I am thinking, *Lord, again?* This journey is hard. I cried, of course, felt the hit, and with prayer and support from everyone I know and love, I am up for the next battle. I asked my radiation oncologist to recommend me for Cyberknife radiation because I thought they would surely treat me now. Ron and I went back to UCSF for what we thought would be with the same physician; however, he was not who we met. Another physician came in to say that after reviewing my films, they felt Gamma Knife Surgery was the appropriate treatment for me. They call it surgery; however, it is radiation. It is high dose radiation that can reach difficult areas, hit the target without affecting surrounding tissue, and only requires one treatment. Due to the scheduled maintenance of the Gamma Knife machine, I was scheduled for treatment about a week later. In the meantime, I was placed on a steroid called Decadron for the headaches. The MD initially felt that the lesions were too small and wondered if the headaches were really coming from the lesions. It was determined that since the Decadron was working, that it must be the lesions.

I continued to work during the next week. I tried to stay focused as much as possible, but the side effects of the medication were affecting my work. I was so irritable that I had to taper off the medication in order to do my job. That was a very long week for me. The side effects along with the anxiety of getting this procedure behind me were not easy. Finally, my appointed day arrived for the procedure. This process involves a neurosurgeon who applies a titanium frame to your skull. This frame locks you into place inside the scanner so that you cannot move during the procedure. It includes a physicist who calculates the amount of Gamma rays to deliver to the affected area, in collaboration with the Gamma Knife MD, on the exact point the radiation is to be delivered to. The nurse prepares the patient with prescribed medications, taking vital signs such as your blood pressure, heart, and respiratory rate, and a technician who delivers the radiation. This is an all-day procedure, yet there is more downtime than the treatment actually takes. Once the neurologist puts the Titanium frame on, I was taken for a repeat scan to compare with the previous scan. They are looking for any changes before they calculated the prescribed dosage, calibrations, and delivery time for my specific treatment. After the scan, I was allowed to eat and visit with Ron and Sister Jackie. Again, I made the decision not to let my children come with us. I did not want them to see their mother with a halo screwed onto her head. I was in protective mode again. So, I asked Sister Jackie, who is my first lady at Beautiful Redeemer, where I am a member, to be there for Ron.

It was really awkward trying to eat around this frame that surrounded my face and head, but I managed as I was surprisingly hungry. The MD came in and told me that the lesions had not changed. There was no increase in size or any more that had developed. She told me that it was determined that my treatment would take eighty minutes in the scanner per their calculations. Now comes the waiting period of approximately two hours while they prepare the prescribed dose of Gamma Rays for me with the precise calibrations into the machine. During this time, all I remember is intermittent sleep, with a light conversation with Ron and Sister Jackie. I received intravenous Decadron, along with IV sedation called Ativan. After two hours, I was taken to the treatment room, locked in place on the table that slides into a tunneled machine that delivers the Gamma Rays. All I remember was the nice soft music playing as I laid there. I thought nothing was happening, everything was so still, and I did not feel anything. Finally, I heard the tech's voice say, "thirty more minutes Karen, you're doing fine." I said, "okay," and I guess I went to sleep. I remember being pulled out of the machine to meet a bunch of smiling faces, some that I had not met before, which included the physicist and one of the associate directors of the Gamma Knife program at UCSF. Ron had the camera clicking, and they all willingly posed for the shots with me. I found out later that they had allowed Ron to take pictures of me during my treatment.

My family was informed of this procedure prior to, all except my mother. She is eighty -six, and I did not want her worrying about me. My daughter wanted to fly home from Phoenix, and my sons were planning to be there. I had friends who wanted to be there. I thought, *My family and friends have been there for me from day one.* I love them all; however, I prayed and prayed for guidance from God. I realized that this is about me, not worrying about hurting anyone's feelings. I made the decision to tell everyone not to come. My daughter to stay in Phoenix, my sons to go to work, my friends, not to come as well. I was accompanied by Ron and my first lady only. This was the right decision for me. I know God hears prayers from wherever you are. I believe that, and I know He heard everyone's. I felt so much peace during the entire day, and I do mean the entire day (7 a.m.–5 p.m.). Yes, I had some sedation; however, God was in that hospital with me. I remember joking at one point, saying I felt like Hannibal Lecter with the equipment I had on my head. Having said that, I realized that Hannibal Lecter had a face mask to prevent him from biting. All I know is that I felt like an alien. I thank God for sister Jackie being able to be there as she was very good for Ron and for me. I must say, however, that when I saw the pictures that Ron was allowed to take during the entire process, I cried. I cried because the pictures looked so barbaric, yet God had kept me in perfect peace. I returned home from the procedure that evening, where I was met by my sons Charles and Markus, who had refused to go to work and were waiting to help me out of the car. I was fed some dinner and sent to bed. I slept a lot the next day, maybe too much. I was told that I could resume my regular activities in twenty-four hours, but when UCSF called to check in on me, they told me to be good to myself and stay home for the rest of the week (this was on Wednesday). I did stay home one more day but decided to go in to work on that Friday. I started out feeling sluggish, but after eating some breakfast, I was good to go. By the end of the day, it started to get rough for me. I felt frazzled and just could not seem to do anything right. After losing my job's cell phone inside a chart that was placed back in the chart rack, I knew it was time to go home.

I had a nice day on Saturday. Ron and I went to see my mother for a short visit, stopped, and bought a pair of limited-edition breast cancer tennis shoes, all before the planned 11:50 movie we attended. The movie provided some lightweight laughter, which was good for me. We left the movies, went to a little local restaurant where we split a burrito, and returned home by 2:30–3 p.m. I felt it was a good day— nothing rushed, nothing urgent, just getting out and enjoying some sun. I even got out and walked my court one time around before I settled down for the rest of the day.

I went to bed that night feeling fine; *however*, I woke up around three with some slight pain behind the eyeballs. It slowly progressed to more severe pain, where my eyes started to run water. I continued to lay there wondering, *Okay, what's going on?* Eventually, I had Ron get up and get me a warm compress to put over my eyes. Once he cut the bathroom light on to get me the compress, I knew something was wrong. The light was so intense that I immediately had to cover my head and have him cut off the lights. I started diagnosing myself and finally decided that Ron should take me to the hospital. I dressed like a blind person with my eyes closed. Going out to the car was scary as the outdoor light was painful even though my face was covered. I got to the emergency room and was waiting for Ron to go in and get help was traumatizing because I needed to get out of the car. Every time I moved, it seemed like the light was able to penetrate my towel. They brought out a wheelchair for me and took me inside. I was triaged, gave them a little history of what had taken place with the Gamma Knife procedure. They placed me in a dark room where I laid for about four hours with IV steroids and IV pain medication on board. I was skeptical about the head scan because I was concerned about too much radiation. They attempted to call my oncologist twice to inquire whether this would be okay. In the meantime, Dr. Wren, a friend, a brother in Christ, member of the same church, who is an orthopedic surgeon, came in and suggested that if the answer was in the scan, I should have it. So, I did and was told it was okay. It was determined that I was being tapered off of the steroid too fast. I was given instructions for the next day and told to call my oncologist for further instructions. I spoke with my oncologist the next day, who gave me verbal instructions but also told me that when I spoke to UCSF, to go by their instructions. I had emailed my MD at UCSF that same night of my ER visit. She responded by email, followed up with a phone call the next day as stated. We went over the tapering regiment. I wrote it out to make sure I got it right this time. I decided that it was best that I stay off work until I completed the steroid therapy. I was doing well, still feeling a little foggy in the head at times, and more sensitive to sound as well.

CHAPTER 8

After the emergency room visit, I felt that I should share with my co-workers what was going on with me. They knew of my previous surgeries and radiation; however, only two knew of the recent diagnosis. I felt that it was time to tell them out of respect. They had been so supportive of me during this journey, and it would not be right if they heard that I was in the ER from other people in the hospital before they heard it from me. I felt better after talking with them. I left the hospital and went on to meet my mother and sister for a breakfast date.

The next step for me was to be rescanned next month (December). The first week to be the MRI of the brain, wait a week, and have a Pet scan of the body for follow-up from the chemo and radiation of the Hilum lymph node.

I had an MRI scan of the brain. The transporter who I met from the previous scans was very nice as usual, very pleasant and talkative. Having the nursing background, I understand that she, as well as the tech who is performing the test, has some knowledge of reading what they see. Upon leaving the test, her comment to me was, "try to have a wonderful Christmas." "I will" was my response. My mind had to go there, *What was she trying to tell me?* I waited twenty-four hours before I called my oncologist's office, telling his secretary that I did not want to wait until next week to get my results. I wanted to know now. He had his nurse tell me to come and see him then. I thought, okay, this cannot be good. He wants to see me instead of telling me on the phone.

I went to see him, and he showed me the results. It showed that the two lesions were still there. I was full of questions, like, did UCSF miss their target? Did I still have cancer? Do I need to repeat the procedure? He could not explain what this meant. I can respect him for that. This is not his area of expertise. He did say that the tumors or lesions did not grow, and there were no other lesions found. He suggested I speak to my MD at UCSF, stating he would be in contact with her as well. I immediately emailed her as this is the fastest way to connect with her. She responded back, saying this was a normal finding. What they looked for was if there were any new lesions noted, or an increase in the previous lesions, or absence of the previous lesions. She felt this is a good sign and stated the lesions would either get smaller, stay the same, or disappear over the next couple of scans that I had. The following week I had a repeat Cat scan of the body. As I was being pulled out of the scanner, the tech said to me, "I am not supposed to say anything, but there is a small spot on the right side. I'm sure they will take care of it. I said, "Okay, thank you," got dressed, and went back to work. I said, "Lord, it's You and me again, and I know that you are going to see me through this. Dr. I can put me back on Avastin again to handle this, and I will be okay." I woke up early the morning of my appointment with my MD to go over my test results. I immediately started asking God for forgiveness. I have continually claimed my healing in the name of Jesus during this whole process and now had accepted what this tech had said to me. Where was my faith? I made it to the appointment, ready to hear what Dr. I had to say. I carried a pen and paper to write things down because now my short-term memory was severely affected by the Gamma Knife radiation. Dr. I walked in with hands in the air, saying, "Everything looks good." I looked at him and said, "What did you say"? He repeated that I was okay. I told him about the incident with the tech. He showed me the report saying the spot he was talking about was inflammation, probably a result of the radiation to that area. Needless to say, I was so happy! We set appointments for repeat scans in three months, and off to work I went. Again, I asked the Lord to forgive me for my anxiety and not trusting fully in Him.

CHAPTER 9

Now I could concentrate more on helping my sister Mallory with her battle with the return of her cancer. She finally let the family in on what was going on with her. She had refused to be treated with chemotherapy a year earlier for a re-occurrence of cancer, stating she did not want any more treatments. She was told that she had a certain time left on this earth; however, she had outlasted their predictions by two years. She now decided that she wanted treatment, and her medical plan physicians did not want to treat her, stating that she refused last year, and now it was too late. I could not believe what I was hearing. How can you refuse to treat a patient just because he or she changes her mind? She had to take this issue to a higher level and appeal their refusal to treat. She was able to get treatment, but she was not feeling comfortable with being treated by these people. She traveled quite a distance to another facility, same medical association, but different people who treated her with radiation in an attempt to shrink her tumors. With the completion of the radiation treatments, she wanted chemotherapy, which the closer facility had refused to give. Now that she won the appeal, they had to treat her. I went with her along with my other sister Mae to most of her appointments for support. We prayed for a favor that everything would work out, and it did. Both sisters were amazed at the different attitude the MD had with her. They both described this physician as uncaring, unprofessional in their previous encounters with her. They felt that during the appeal process, the higher

authorities must have spoken with her, which caused her to check her attitude. I say it was God who intervened and will maintain that thought.

My sister and I are Christians and are strong believers of His *Word*. We understand that God will allow us to be tested. Look at the book of Job. He went through so much, not because he was a bad person. In fact, he was faithful to God in everything that he did, yet, he lost everything. His friends thought he must have done something so unforgivable because of all that he lost. Instead of supporting their friend, they were judging him. Well, we know how the book ended—God put Job's friend in check, had Job pray for his friends, and Job ending up with double of everything he lost. The point is this: we have to have unwavering faith in everything we go through, trusting God's Word, regardless of what man tells us.

This brings me to an incident I experienced with a physician at UCSF. I went to see a physician there to see if I qualified for a clinical trial study for triple-negative breast cancer. She was recommended to me by my second surgeon. Apparently, she is well known in her area of expertise and only sees patients twice a week and travels giving lectures the rest of the week. Because of this, it took a long time to book an appointment with her; however, her secretary stated this was quite fast for me. Her office required a lot of paperwork to be faxed to them ahead of time for review—the same procedure with the Cyberknife appointment. One thing I can say for UCSF is, they are very thorough. They require every scan on disk, every pathology report, every lab result, etc., that has been taken. I understood why once I had my visit. The physician goes over every one of the tests in the correct sequence of events with you, then proceed with why you came for your visit. This particular physician reviewed everything with me. She then proceeded to tell me that it did not matter what treatment I was given by my physician. She stated that I had three or five years to live and could not believe that my physicians had not told me this. I felt my eyes get really big, and I proceeded to repeat everything she said to me to make sure I heard her right. I cannot explain in words exactly how I was feeling at that time, but it was not good. I looked at her and asked her if she had any patients who were believers. She stated to me, "yes, and they actually live longer." I said, "Well, *I am* a believer, and I refused to accept what she was saying. After all that she said to me regarding my situation, stage IV cancer with metastasis, she then said that I did not fit her criteria for a clinical trial study, that I was not sick enough for her study. The appointment ended with me to make an appointment with her in six weeks for a follow up with her secretary. She gave me a hug and was gone. I thought, why do I need to see her for a follow-up appointment? There is absolutely no reason to see this person who bluntly told me what she did. I know that God gives man knowledge. I am a professional, and I have seen predictions by physicians come true. But also, I am a child of God, and I know that He has the last say in everything. He is the real Physician, and I believe I am not finished on this earth until He says so. I understand that for me to be absent in this body is to be present with the Lord. However, I believe that I still have work to do here and that God is not finished with me yet.

Three months had passed and it was time for a repeat total body scan as well as an MRI of my brain. I admit this is not a good feeling, as I was experiencing all kinds of emotions. Emotions as, *okay, let's get this over with* to *Lord, I don't want to go through this again*. I know that I am going to be looking for some sort of sign by what the technician does or does not say. Well, I had the body scan done first, a week before the MRI of the brain. Prior to the scan, I talked a lot to myself and to God, declaring my health, being persistent and consistent, so I thought. On the other hand, my flesh wanted to convince me that the cancer was back because I was having a lot of aches and pains. I went for the scan, prayed silently during the procedure, wishing it to be over fast because I do not like lying in that tube. As I was leaving, the same tech who did the procedure last time said to me, "I like your smile; you just keep on smiling, okay?" I said, "Alright, I will," and left for home. I decided not to call my oncologist this time to get the results. I was scheduled the following week for the MRI and opted to wait. I must say that the wait was not comfortable, but I had to believe that I was okay. I thought Dr. I would call me if something was wrong because he knew how I felt the last time and did not wait until my appointment with him to get the results. The following week I had an MRI of the brain. It was an early morning appointment, which I like because I was the first appointment of the day, not following behind another patient. I went on to work after the procedure, trying to stay busy. The technician this time was very nice and pleasant; however, he said nothing that I could even try to decipher the possible results. All he said was, "Have a good day." This was all he should have said, to be honest, because it is not the technician's place to say anything. I was at my work station when my primary MD walked up to me and asked me if I had a procedure that day because my name showed up on the computer under his patient list. I confirmed that I did and that I had another one the week before and was waiting on the results. He stated that he would follow up and let me know. I did not hear from him before I left for home. My phone rang at 7:00 p.m. that evening, and it was him telling me that my MRI of the brain was negative. The lesions were gone. Needless to say, I was so happy; however, the first thing that came out of my mouth was, "What about the Pet Scan that I took the week prior to the MRI?" He stated that he could not pull up the results of that test because his name was not on it. He would inquire and get back to me, but he wanted me to have the news about the MRI. I was grateful for his call and immediately thanked the Lord. I still had two more days, and I was determined not to call Dr. I before my appointment. I was going to trust that everything was alright, yet, my flesh again was trying to get the better of me. I was declaring my healing externally, but internally, I was struggling with mixed emotions. I know the Word of God tells us not to waiver in our faith, be steadfast in His Word. I had to repent because of this. I was really hard on myself because I should know by now that it is in God's hands, and worrying is not of God. Well, I went for my appointment, and while I was sitting in the waiting room, Dr. I had come out of an exam room, walked over to me, and said, "your scan looks great." I said out loud, "Thank you, Lord!" There was a gentleman sitting across from me who heard me say that, and he asked me, "What is the Lord to you?" I said to him, "I am His child!" with a lot of enthusiasm. He came back with, "So am I." I went into the exam room where Dr. I and talked and discussed the plan of care and when my next scan/MRI would be scheduled. The plan is to have my mammogram and MRI of the left breast in one month, which would be my one-year check-up. My follow-up body scan and brain MRI would be in four months instead of three. I left his office with a sense of peace and thanksgiving in my heart and went back to work.

CHAPTER 10

Reflections

When I think of everything I have been through in the past three years, I know that God has and will always be there for me. From the beginning, the way I found the lump. I had not been checking my breast like I should every month. I did it when I thought about it, which was maybe every two or three months. Yet that morning, I was led by the Holy Spirit to place my hand right on top of the lump after reading my Bible, praying, and meditating as usual. The fact that I was able to get the ultrasound that same day was by the grace of God. Everything was working out for my good, even though it was a bad situation. The next thing I recall was the support of family and friends who were there. It was like everyone had assignments the morning of my first surgery that just went so smoothly. My girlfriend Cheryl came from Sacramento one hour away) to spend the night with me. Her assignment was to take Cameron, my nephew, to school that morning before coming to the hospital. She and my girlfriend Yolanda together were to take Ron to breakfast while I was in for a procedure prior to the surgery. My other girlfriend Linda and her husband, Rob, went to keep my mother company and distracted while I had surgery. My girlfriend Berney was my nurse in the pre-op unit. She not only was my nurse but prayed with Ron and me at the bedside before my procedure. This support allowed my family members to wait and come closer to the time of surgery, which was three hours later from the time I had to arrive. I remember waking up and getting dressed to go home to find another friend Wanda there, helping me put on my shoes. I was told later that my girl Diane was there with the family in the waiting room; however, I did not get a chance to see her. God showed me so much love through the support, as I mentioned, along with my family. My family is so big that they can fill up a waiting room by themselves.

Over the recovery period, I received so many cards, flowers, plants, dinner, fruit, and visits from so many people that I was overwhelmed. I even had a surprise visit from my cousin Uri who flew in from Memphis to see me. I thought this is so special. Uri is the same age as my son Charles. We developed this bond while Uri was in law school at Gonzaga University. Ron and I were visiting our son Ron Jr in Washington state and decided to look Uri up to say Hi. We initially thought that young people do not want to be bothered with old folks (smile), so we won't take up much of his time. The visit was wonderful, and it led to many phone calls and check-ups on him, making sure he was okay. He was threatened by the skinheads while he was running for office to represent Gonzaga's law school. This led to numerous phone calls to the University from all family members insisting they protect Uri at all cost. The University ended up moving Uri back on campus for his protection. He graduated from the University, and I might add that he is a successful, humble lawyer, whom I am proud to call my "little cousin."

I forgot to mention my cousins James and Michelle flew in from Southern California prior to my surgery to see me, and I was treated with James' special T-cakes that we all love. The fact that their visit was just for forty-four hours was amazing! They flew in on a Saturday morning, came in cooking. Family members came over in which we partook of some good eating, and they flew out the next day.

My daughter in law Teoni informed me after the fact that she had participated in a Susan G Komen "Breast Cancer Walk" in my honor. This event was after my family had already participated in a breast cancer walk given in honor of "Faith Fancher," who was an award-winning journalist. Faith passed away from breast cancer in 2003. At this particular event, an unknown sponsor paid for me to have a booth to sell my books which I did while my family participated in the walk. I believe my nephew Devin actually was at the head of the pack of the race. I don't remember what number he placed; however, he did quite well.

My niece Alethea made a collage with pictures, including a family picture of everyone who participated in the breast cancer walk, one of my book signing events, with words of encouragement. It still hangs on my bedroom wall to this day. I felt so loved!

Another act of love was this. My family had not seen my first cousins on my father's side since I was a little kid. I was around ten years of age. Well, my aunt Lois in Arizona told them about my diagnosis. I remember receiving a card in the mail from cousin Diane. It was not only a card saying hello, but a card with her telling me about Christ. She did not know that I was a believer. How could she? We had not been in touch with each other for over thirty years! I responded to her card, thanking her for reaching out and letting her know that "yes, I have accepted Jesus as my Lord and Savior." I also received a call from her other two sisters, Barbara and Carol, both with encouraging and supportive words. We corresponded back and forth for a while by phone or mail. Finally, Barbara asked if it would be okay if she came for a visit, even if it was for twenty-four hours. I was so touched by this. We set a date for the visit, which would be in between the start of my second round of chemotherapy. Not only did Barbara come, but Diane and Carol came as well. It was such a wonderful visit to see them after all these years. We lost contact with them because my siblings and I were not raised by my father, and we only saw them when we were little, visiting my father in the summer months. Those visits became fewer and fewer; therefore, we did not see our cousins. We still stay in touch by email and occasional phone calls. I invited them to meet me in Arizona last year in October so we could spend time with our two surviving aunts on our father's side. That visit was wonderful, as they were with me when I shared the news to my Aunt Lois about my diagnosis with brain cancer. The visit was good for my daughter, Brienne, as well. This was her first visit with them as we all stayed at her home. We ate a lot, shopped, went to church, and just spent some quality time together. This is family. This is *Love!*

I decided that I wanted to share my story and to speak out for breast cancer awareness. I have been a speaker at one of the Susan G Komen Foundation events in San Francisco. I participated in a short Marathon sponsored by the same foundation while on a Jazz cruise. I ran into a former church member while on the cruise who encouraged me and walked with me. I must say I was much slower than most, but it felt good to complete it. Thank you, Yoshiko. I have shared my testimonies at numerous functions while promoting my first book. I have been a speaker at the Iscah Uzza Foundation, which was created by a young lady with a dream that came to manifest itself in a big way. She combined her love for fashion with supporting men and women diagnosed with breast and prostate cancer. Her proceeds helped organizations with financial and emotional assistance to those patients in need of support. I was so surprised and thankful to be presented with a personalized handmade quilt in my honor at one of her events. I was so touched. She invited me to participate in a cancer survivor calendar, which I did with my son Charles. Thank you, Kamari, for following your dreams and helping so many people. It was a lot of fun to do, yet for a serious cause.

Through all of this, I thank God because He is worthy to be praised. His *Word* tells us that we are going to have trials and tribulations. It is not His desire that we give up but that we persevere. II Peter tells us that after we have suffered a while, He will perfect, establish, strengthen, and settle us. It is not His desire that we give up, but depend and trust Him to be there for us. He is able to heal us miraculously or through man. He is the God of all comfort, and I will always continue to look to Him as the real Physician. No man knows the time, the hour, the day, the month, or the year of our departure from this earth but God. It is up to Him and only Him.

Lord, I will continue to declare my healing; Amen!

PART

CHAPTER 11

8/2020

Here it is six years later, and my journey has continued. So much has happened, and so much has changed—Cliff note version (unless the Holy Spirit directs me to elaborate).

I have been divorced for five years; my sister Mallory transitioned on August 21st, 2015, my mother on March 10th, 2017, my baby brother James, on May 7th, 2019, and my sister Mae, on February 13th, 2020. We are in the middle of a global pandemic (Corona Virus or COVID-19), where over 170,000 people have lost their lives. We are required to self-distance ourselves as much as possible, staying six feet apart, with a "shelter in place" mandate, and to wear masks when we leave our homes for any reason. Racial injustice is at an all-time high, with riots going on in many states. People are angry over the witnessing of a murder of an African American by a knee of a police officer to his neck.

Let me not forget about the fires that are destroying thousands of acres of land and peoples' homes. We are already wearing masks because of the pandemic; however, now we need to protect ourselves from the smoke that is blanketing our environment. There is news coverage of depression and suicidal ideations of some people who are having a difficult time handling these crises. People have lost their jobs, their income, their homes, and their medical coverage. We are now in the middle of the Presidential campaign with candidates doing what they do best, blaming each other for the situations we find ourselves in. This is a lot to absorb mentally for a faith-based person, let alone for someone who does not have a relationship with God.

Since my divorce, I have had a few more episodes with my health, the mediastinum chest area), a second event to the brain (this time on the right), and a lymph node.

I moved in with my son on March 7th, 2014. Shortly after moving in, I learned that my granddaughter Naya needed heart surgery. She had been under medical care for a heart murmur and headaches. I was there for the consultation appointment with the cardiac surgeon along with my son Charles and daughter in law Teonie (Naya's parents). It was decided that she would have the procedure at the end of the current school year. Before Naya's surgery, my son Charles needed to have thyroid surgery, which he had been avoiding for a while. We had a discussion that he needed to address his health issue first to be there for Naya. He had been walking around with a lump in his neck the size of a golf ball. An anesthesiologist discovered it during a surgical procedure to repair a torn Achilles tendon that occurred during an adult baseball league game. Well, the surgery was successful, and the pathology report was negative for cancer. Thank You, Lord!

Prior to Naya's surgery, I had my regular scheduled MRI check-up and was found to have a new brain lesion on the right. Needless to say, my faith was challenged. I kept this news from the family because we needed to put all of our attention on Naya.

My daughter, Bri, who now lives in Virginia, flew in, and my sisters Mae and Mallory along with my mom reserved a hotel room for two nights to be closer to the hospital where Naya would be. They live over fifty miles north of me. All the while we were there for Naya, I was actively working on my own behalf secretly on the phone with my insurance company, trying to speed up the authorization process for my consultation with UCSF. It was hard to keep what I was doing to myself, having to share with a few of my family members what was going on with me. I did not tell Charles or Teonie until Naya's surgery was over, and she was stable.

I headed back home, where my journey continued. This time it was a different physician at UCSF and a different technique. Instead of the titanium halo, it was a bite block in which a mold of my mouth was made. It was like dental work. This personalized bite block would fit in my mouth, connect to the scanner, and lock me in place to the machine. Instead of one treatment, this required five treatments because the lesion was larger. Different people took me to my treatments. Again there was sister Jackie and Pastor Mike to take me for my initial treatment plan. As I sat in the back seat, I felt the need to have them call their son Andrew who was away at college. I know Drew to be a young, powerful man of God whose prayers reach deep within my soul. When sister Jackie called Drew, he was still in his dorm room. He told his mom he didn't really know why he was delayed but then understood. He was held up by the Holy Spirit to pray with me along with his parents.

My recovery was slow, as we learned from last time not to wean off the steroid too fast. I kept a scheduled chart on the refrigerator door with the dosage for the days and weeks to follow. Anyone who has been on steroids for a long length of time can understand when I say it is *no* fun. The mood swings, anxiety, irritability, the "moon face," and weight gain, all side effects I experienced. Again, my family and friends were there for me. The recovery time felt so lonely in spite of people being there. There is still that mental/spiritual part that was between God and me to work through. I was a fighter, and I am a warrior. I would declare to myself, "I am healed by the stripes of Jesus," regardless of how bad I was feeling. I tried my best not to show Markus how bad I was feeling. I would walk up and down the court where we lived during the day, trying to gain my strength, playing my gospel music.

This point in my life was extremely hard for me. Due to personal reasons that I will not get into, I had walked away from a twenty-seven-year marriage (of a thirty-year relationship)—a marriage that had affected me physically, mentally, and spiritually, which is the reason for such a long pause in my writing. It took a lot of prayer and soul searching to come to peace with my decision to just walk away.

Where I could recite the names of chemotherapy drugs to the incidents with the exact years prior to 2015, I had subconsciously blotted out. I no longer wanted to keep track. I stopped keeping my records of scan reports in my binder. I believe this to be a mental safety mechanism for me. I was not in denial; I just felt the need to focus on the present, not the past. Never forgetting what God had done for me or brought me through, but to cherish the present day and thank Him for the "now."

CHAPTER 12

After recovering from the second brain cancer episode, I returned to work. I lived with Mark for one complete year. On March 7th, 2015, I moved into my own condo that I purchased in the same neighborhood as Mark. Living in my own place for one month, my place of employment shut its doors. Doctor's Medical Center closed after fifty years of service to a community of 250,000 residents. Now, this community will only have a fifty bed Kaiser hospital that is there to service their own members.

A lot of nurses were already working part-time at other hospitals. I, on the other hand, was holding on to the faith that some company was going to come along and bail us out like so many times before. I was even involved in going to city council meetings speaking on behalf of the hospital and the employees but to no avail this time. No more "Rams in the bush," No more bailouts from other hospitals or state assistance for our financial problems.

The hospital held a job fair for the employees in an attempt to help as many of us to find employment. I had not needed a resume in thirty-six years! I had to get help, so I reach out to my pastor (Michael Gonzales of Beautiful Redeemer Ministries) and Goddaughter Keandra for some assistance. Between the two of them, my resume was quite good, and I had an awesome cover letter as well.

Praise report: Doctors Hospital closed on April 15th, 2015, and I started work at Kaiser Oakland on May 18th, 2015. God is *so* good! I only had to pay out of pocket for two months before my current medical coverage became active. What I also will mention is that Doctors Medical Center had changed our insurance coverage while still in operation about a year prior to closing. They did this in an attempt to save money, switching us over to a Kaiser plan from Blue Cross coverage. This meant I had to switch my oncologist with whom I had established a relationship, as well as my primary medical physician, who I had for years. I was very fond of both of them, which made it very difficult to gain trust and establish a relationship all over again. While I have had a change in my oncologist twice since becoming a Kaiser employee, my primary medical physician happens to be the spouse of my oncologist at Doctors. I was told that this physician was not taking new patients; however, this MD did accept me with her busy load. Look at God!

CHAPTER 13

Becoming acclimated to the Kaiser family as an employee, my journey continues. I was still being monitored every three months with scans, MRIs, and doctors' appointments. My sister Mallory was continuing with her appointments and tests as well, or so I thought. We were out to lunch, my mom, Mal, and sister Mae at Fenton's Restaurant. We were really fond of ice creameries. It was like treating ourselves either before or after treatments or doctor appointments. I happened to ask Mal what and when was the next treatment plan scheduled for her. I wanted to check for any conflicts in our schedules so that I could be there for her. We tried to support each other as much as possible. Instead of an immediate answer, there was a long pause before she proceeded to inform us that there would be no more treatments. She had made a decision to enroll in the hospice program. I cannot remember how long the silence lasted. It felt like forever. I believe for the first time, we saw how tired she was and no longer wanted to fight.

It seems like time really sped up after Mallory's announcement. I went with her to a lawyer to arrange to have a trust written up. I decided to do my own at the same time. This was difficult to do, however necessary. What I did not realize until much later was that while I had excused myself to go to the restroom, Mal had told the lawyer that she needed her paperwork completed within two weeks. Sure enough, shortly after she and a girlfriend went to pick up her completed trust, she passed away. I do not remember the exact amount of time, but her battle ended, and she went on to be with the Lord.

CHAPTER 14

Over the course of the next two years, I was treated with Cyberknife radiation to the mediastinal area, which is in the chest area. This would be my first treatment at a Kaiser facility. It required five treatments which were scheduled three days one week and two days the next week, with a day off in between each session. This allowed me to work on the off-day since I had no side effects from the radiation. This radiation oncologist, who was to treat me, was one of my sister's physician. As we were about to end the consultation meeting with her (my son Mark and my girlfriend Yolanda were present), I shared with her that I was Mallory's sister, and I trusted her treatment plan. My sister spoke very highly of her, and I came to realize why. She was the only one of Mal's physician I did not meet. This led Dr. G. to finally admit that she almost walked back out the door, thinking I was Mallory when she knew she had passed. I have been told Mal and I look alike all of my life (smile).

This time in my life, I am working in a new environment where I know no one really knows my story, not even my boss. Yet, I had to speak with her to get the time off. I was hesitant about letting co-workers into this part of my life. I didn't know them, and they didn't know me. I had been at one job for thirty-six and a half years, where people saw and knew me before and after my diagnosis. They knew me with hair and without hair and then with hair again, although I chose to keep it short. For so many reasons I can not explain, I was skeptical about sharing. This was a new culture, a new environment that I needed to adapt to. Then there was Jinny, my office mate who joined Kaiser one month after me. She came a month later; however, it was a transfer from another Kaiser facility in Oregon. There was a connection, a friendship that developed, one with respect that lead me to open up to her. I eventually started to mention a few facts about myself to others, however, not to the degree within this book.

CHAPTER 15

During the same two years, my mother, who had been suffering from dementia, passed. She fell outside of a major department store, sustaining a fractured hip. This required surgery, which she never recovered from and never returned home. My mom's passing was hard for us all, but more so with my sister Mae because she was my mom's caregiver. They were the closest as Mae never married and lived next door to my mother. She had moved my mother into her place as her health deteriorated approximately three years before her passing. I would try and keep my mother for at least one day a week to give Mae a break. Taking care of an elderly parent with dementia is quite difficult. It hurts to watch your loved one who took care of you become the child. There's the role reversal. Mae took on that role and did a wonderful job. I am not saying it was easy for her, but she did it. I will always remember my mother as a strong, loving person before dementia slowly manifested itself. She loved God, loved people, and loved her clothes. She went to church always dressed beautifully, from her suit to the matching shoes, purse, and hat. She always had a smile on her face, and she loved to kiss people hello out of love. She had the gift of sewing, making beautiful quilts for the entire family—every one of us, including grandchildren, owned at least one of her creations. When mom passed, it was the most difficult for Mae. She had lost her best friend and felt lost, not really being able to move forth with her own life, no matter how hard I tried to encourage her to do so. It was like she was frozen and would always say, "you don't understand. I lived with mom for seventy years."

I finally convinced Mae to take a trip two years later to visit our nephew Joseph who now lives in Texas. Mae raised Joe, who was just a toddler when he came to live with her, joining his older brother Devin, who Mae had since he was nine months old. We would also get to meet our great-nephew Jodie for the first time. We had a wonderful time with Joseph showing us around the town, eating good food, enjoying nephew Jodie. We attended Joel Osteen's megachurch that Sunday for Mother's Day, followed by an awesome brunch that Joseph has arranged. It seemed strange, but also a very nice experience to see Joe as a young man and now a father, picking us up and driving us around. It had been a few years since we had seen him as he went to live with his father in Louisiana as a teen. From there, we flew to Virginia to spend time with my daughter Bri. This was what we needed, for Mae to get away, and a break for me as well, being in between tests, scans, and doctor appointments.

CHAPTER 16

We flew back to California, arriving late in San Francisco. By the time I dropped Mae off at home, it was probably close to midnight. Driving home, Mae called me to say she noticed a card was stuck in her door with a message to call this person who had placed the card on the door. The note said that this person has some information about our brother James (Stevie). By the time I reached home and called Mae back, she had informed me that our brother had passed away in a hospital. I was initially frozen in my thoughts but quickly made the call to the person on the card. This person had informed me that they had not seen James in a few days, which was strange for him, and made some inquiries at the encampment area where he was residing. I was told that the police had been there earlier asking questions about anyone knowing James. Everyone there denied they knew him, thinking he was in trouble. The encampment family did reveal that he had been complaining of severe abdominal pain. With that information, phone calls were made to various hospitals searching for James, which led them to find out that James had passed away. I was given the phone number of the coroner's office, where it was confirmed to me that James had indeed passed. He had a ruptured aneurysm, which was causing severe pain, along with sepsis and multi-organ failure. As I am writing this, there are tears flowing because not only did my brother die, he did so with no family around and in all that pain. Another fact that was realized is that James had passed before Mae and I left on our trip to Texas and Virginia. There was no one there for James during his crisis. No one could explain how he happened to end up in a hospital so far away from his encampment site. Regardless of the fact that James was estranged from his family, he was still our brother. Saying our goodbyes to James was heartbreaking as Mae and I made his final arrangements. I still see the picture of his face, which I choose not to elaborate on, but is ingrained in me forever.

CHAPTER 17

Moving forward with life the best we can, we head into December of 2019. Me still trying to encourage Mae to move on with her life. We discussed her selling her homes, putting her belongings in storage, and staying with me until she decided on where she wanted to move. She no longer needed to try and maintain two households living alone and complaining about her neighbors. She would entertain the idea; however, she never could or would move forth. There would always be an excuse, but she would say, "I am moving; I just don't know where."

I did finally convince her to make a doctor's appointment because I would always ask her why she would hold onto her abdominal area with certain movements. She would always brush it off, saying, "It's nothing." Well, that nothing led to blood, test, X-rays, scans proving to be suspicious for malignancy. I took her for a surgical consultation appointment, which led to a procedure in San Francisco to confirm the diagnosis of pancreatic CA. She was diagnosed by one physician as stage II, while another stated stage IB. The plan was to go for a cure, so we agreed to go for the "big guns" (chemotherapy) followed by surgery in that order. My daughter, Bri, and nephew Devin, who were still in town for Christmas, joined us for the oncology appointment, where they were able to get their questions answered.

We made it through the Christmas season with plans for treatments to start in January of this year (2020). My scan, which was due, showed a positive lymph node that needed treatment. I decided to ask for a consultation for Mae to see if she could be treated with Cyberknife as well. I had researched the treatment and was hopeful, thinking that this would be tolerated much better than the current plan.

My son Charles drove us both to our appointments with the same MD who had treated me the last time. Charles was to be the second set of ears and to take notes. The physician agreed with the others for Mae's plan and gave her reasons. I, on the other hand, would begin my treatments, which happened to be five sessions again.

Here it is again, two sisters being treated for their individual issues, only this time instead of Mallory and I, it's Mae and me. I was still able to work in between my treatment days as before. I had different family and friends to drive me, not wanting to be a burden. There was Berney, Yolanda, Cheryl, and my son Markus. Mae offered to drive me once, even though she knew I would not let her. That's just the type of person she was, always putting others before herself.

I believe I completed my treatments before Mae started her first round of chemo. I remembered sitting there the whole time with Berney paying us a short visit. I was not going to leave her. I needed to be instructed on the care of her take-home infusion bag, which was part of her treatment plan, and to make sure she understood it. I would be given her the injections that she needed for the next four to five days following the chemo because she could not do it herself.

The chemotherapy was brutal on Mae. She would only stay with me for one day after the first infusion, insisting on being in her own place. It was approximately twenty-four hours later before she started feeling the effects of the meds—nausea, vomiting, constipation, listlessness, and lack of appetite. It took lots of encouragement to get her to force the fluids. I would stop by every day after work to check on her. She never quite bounced back before the next cycle was scheduled. This time Devin was in town to take her to her appointment, with me dropping in for a quick check-in.

Mae kept saying to me that she just felt different. I explained that from my own experience, with each session, the build-up of chemo in your system makes you weaker. I had made up in my mind on this particular Friday after work, and I would bring her some Won Ton soup from a restaurant that she likes and at least encourage her to drink the broth. When I arrived, I saw how weak she looked and immediately sat her down with the broth. It took a threat from me with going to the hospital before she would drink the coffee cup full of broth. It wasn't long after she finished drinking when she immediately had to run to the restroom. Well, she didn't quite make it to the bathroom in time, and the incident required that we put her in the shower. She appeared more comfortable after the shower, clean, and able to sleep. I had made a decision that I was not going home anytime soon. I would periodically have her take a few sips of water, but right then, she needed to rest. After sleeping for two hours, everything went downhill once she woke up. She was in a fog, trying to get out of bed, turning over a water glass that was on her nightstand, which eventually hit the floor. I knew it was time to call 911. She kept saying "no"; however, I wasn't listening to her. She literally pulled me to the kitchen to make sure that the door that leads to the outside was double-locked before she would cooperate with me to sit on the living room sofa to wait for the paramedics. When I called the EMS, I requested no sirens due to the hour of the evening, but to come quickly, explaining the situation. They arrived, it seemed immediately, took down the necessary information, and proceeded to place her on the gurney.

I locked her house up after gathering a few of her personal items she requested and joined her at the hospital.

In my mind, my sister was going to get hydrated intravenously, rest awhile, and then I would take her to my house for the weekend. I knew the drill; I have been there myself, needing to go and have IV hydration before I would begin to feel better. My sister Mallory had the same experiences needing hydration, more than one can take in orally. It did not dawn on me once that Mae would never come home again. She was pronounced a few hours later, as I stood watching from the doorway of her room while the ER staff worked emergently on her. I felt like I was having a bad dream. This was not happening. We had faith, we prayed, we declared the Word of God in this situation. Yet, this was not God's plan for Mae. My sister passed from a heart attack.

CHAPTER 18

I am feeling quite numb, yet, I need to start making funeral arrangements for Mae. I lost my big sister, who I was very close to. The emotions that I am feeling are not describable at this time. Out of the six children my mom bore, Mae and I were the closest in our adult lives. Mal, Mae, and I had sibling issues just like any other family, but the support we had for one another, no one can dispute.

Right after the beautiful homegoing celebration for Mae, I left for Southern Ca. to spend time with relatives, James and Michelle, a much-needed escape. This time away for a few days allowed me to pray, to cry, to meditate, and to rest in God. I was also able to connect with relatives on my father's side and spend some quality time with them as well as having a breakfast date with goddaughter Keandra.

Upon my return home, I felt I needed to get to work; I needed to stay busy. I did not want to have too much time on my hands to think. I would find myself picking up the phone to call Mae to see how she was doing or sharing some piece of news with her. I realized that I really had not had time to grieve.

When I called my manager to discuss when I would return to work, I was told that I had to make a choice to either return to work or stay off work until April 7th. This was because of the COVID-19 pandemic outbreak and was the date that was enforced if you had a pre-existing illness. During this time, the rules were changing all of the time. This shelter in place was just getting started, and I was initially told that I could not wear a mask in the hallways at work. If I felt uncomfortable at all, not wearing a mask to stay home. I decided that I would take time off and shelter in place. Over the course of the next two weeks, my manager would occasionally email me with the latest updates of the ever-present changing rules. I found that staying home was not good for me mentally or spiritually. I had to keep fighting negative thoughts of fear, doubts, feeling alone, not being a burden to anyone with my struggles. I cried a lot, mainly at night, which was the worst time for me. I had to constantly tell myself that God would not give me more than I could handle, that I am more than a conqueror, that I am an overcomer, and that no weapon formed against me shall prosper. I would remind myself that I am a child of the Most High God. His eyes are on me, and His ears are opened to my prayers, that when I cry out, He hears me and delivers me from all of my troubles. I would question myself on the scripture that says, "perfect love cast out fear." Does this mean that I do not love You, Lord, because I am fearful right now? I have the scripture John 14:27, "Peace I leave you, My peace I give you," on my wall over my headboard. So I ask, "where is my peace, Lord?" The *scripture* that says God gives His beloved sleep (Psalm 127:2), so why am I not able to sleep?

CHAPTER 19

This has been a constant struggle for me as I have returned to work. I know the struggles that I have are not unique. There is a pandemic going on, and people are dying from it. People are depressed, lonely, scared, losing their jobs, and some, their homes. Yet, in all of this, I will encourage myself in the Lord. I will make every attempt to stand on God's Word, that He will never leave me nor forsake me. He knows what is going on, for He is all-knowing, all-powerful, and ever-present. This is a faith walk, believing without seeing, trusting that all things work together for good to those who love God and are called according to His purpose. Therefore, I will encourage myself with the Word of God because His promises are "Yes and Amen." That in everything, I will give thanks for this is the will of God. I am not going to ask God why does life have to be so hard. His Word tells us that the secret things belong to Him. Those things which are revealed belong to us. I must remember that what we see here on earth is temporary, and that which is unseen is eternal. Therefore, I will walk with the faith that is required of me, for without faith, God says it is impossible to please Him. I realize that God does not have to prove Himself to me. No, He showed Himself strong to His chosen people. He parted the Red Sea. He poured water from a rock. He fed His people with manna from heaven and quail. He opened up the earth and swallowed men alive. He spoke through a burning bush. His people's clothes did not wear out after traveling for forty years in the wilderness. Yet through all of this, His people complained. God loved us so much, wanting a relationship with us, His people, that He gave His Son as a replacement for our sins. God did all of these things and so much more, yet there is so much hatred, bitterness, selfishness, pride, jealousy, envy, lying, backbiting love of self, money, and fame. Do I really have the nerve to say, "I am angry at You God for what You did or did not do for me?" I think not! So, let me say this, life has not been easy, yet God blessed me to be here through all of this that is written. I pray that my story will encourage readers to continue to put one foot in front of the other, to wrap themselves in faith by believing God's Word. We need to know God's Word before we can have faith in His Word. Surround yourself with positive praying people. People who will lift you up, not tear you down. People who will remind you of His words and His promises. His Word says to comfort others in the way we have been comforted. I know no other way than to tell my story in the hope to encourage others to wrap themselves up in faith and trust that God is always with us.

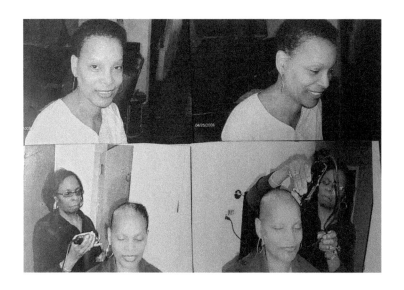

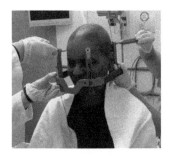

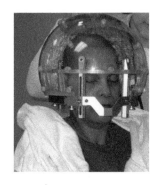

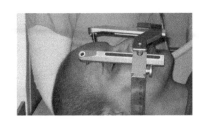

Case Manager Karen Bolden Speaks At Annual Susan Komen Foundation Conference

Last month DMC's own Karen Bolden, RN/Case Manager *(pictured below)*, was invited to speak at the annual Komen Foundation SF Conference. The Foundation, which provides funding for breast cancer prevention and services, invited Karen to share "Her Story: Personal Experiences with Late Sta Diagnosis." Karen, who is a five-tin cancer survivor, inspired hope and courage among many of the dozens conference attendees.

"Your staff from the registration to the Doctors were courteous and helpful. 10 out of

–June 21, 2013 Ou Center Feedba

"Iam very pleased that we have been selected as a recipient of th

ABOUT THE AUTHOR

This is Karen's second book. The first one is called *Karen's Anointed Expressions Presents "Blessed."*

She is the mother of three grown children, along with raising a nephew for eleven years. She has worked as a Registered Nurse for the past forty years in different positions, from Medical-Surgical to Intensive Care, and now Case Management.

Karen hopes her story will empower other cancer patients to walk in the faith of God's Word to assist them through their journey.

CPSIA information can be obtained
at www.ICGtesting.com
Printed in the USA
LVHW070001280321
682703LV00022B/1628

9 781637 690307